MANATEES

Our Vanishing Mermaids

by M. Timothy O'Keefe

Larsen's Outdoor Publishing

ISBN 0-936513-43-8

Library of Congress 93-79803

Published by:

LARSEN'S OUTDOOR PUBLISHING
2640 Elizabeth Place
Lakeland, FL 33813
(813) 644-3381
(813) 644-3288 fax

PRINTED IN THE UNITED STATES OF AMERICA

7 8 9 10

"For in the end, we will conserve only what we love, we will love only what we understand, and we will understand only what we are taught."

Baba Dioum
African naturalist

DEDICATION

To the manatees themselves: you who have developed such a complete and natural harmony with your environment. We humans aware of your accomplishment can only view you with awe...and envy.

M. Timothy O'Keefe
Aspiring Manatee

ABOUT THE AUTHOR

M. Timothy O'Keefe has been a diver for more than 30 years. He is an award-winning author of Diving to Adventure and co-author of Fish & Dive Florida & The Keys and Fish & Dive the Caribbean, Vol. 1, listed in the Resource Directory at the back of this book. His articles and photographs have also appeared in numerous publications worldwide, including National Geographic Society books, Time-Life Books, Rodale's Scuba Diving, SCUBA Times, Diving & Snorkeling, Caribbean Travel & Life, Newsweek, Travel & Leisure, and more.

Tim holds a PhD from the University of North Carolina at Chapel Hill and is a professor in the School of Communication at the University of Central Florida in Orlando, where he established the journalism program. He is a member of the Outdoor Writers Association of America (OWAA), the Society of American Travel Writers (SATW) and a past president of the Florida Outdoor Writers Association (FOWA).

CONTENTS

MANATEES

INTRODUCTION

Manatees and elephants.

The two animals are continents apart in geography and appearance. Yet scientists say the manatee and elephant probably not only share a common ancestry, they possibly share the same bleak future: extinction.

In both situations, the causes are the same, man's interference with the animals' environment. Several aspects in particular have combined to aggravate the manatees' situation. Their habitat has been reduced by the filling of tidal marshes and inshore grass flats to create more land for homes and shopping centers. The loss of traditional grazing and breeding ground forced the animals out into areas where more frequent contact with man was inevitable.

At the same time, the ever increasing popularity of boating also impacted the manatee population; according to the Florida Department of Environmental Protection, collisions with boats annually account for about 24 percent of all manatee deaths.

The manatee population today is estimated at between 1,800 and 2,200 animals. No one knows for certain how

MANATEES

Blue Spring was crowded with weekend boats and bathers in the early 1970s before it became a state park.

many manatees lived in Florida at the turn of the century, but many have assumed it was considerably higher.

In the meantime, Florida's human population continues to mushroom unchecked. Florida is now the fourth most populous state. Unless the manatee's critical environment is protected, the animals will never bounce back meaningfully. They are likely to remain precariously balanced on the razor edge of survival or be reduced to such small numbers that a viable population is impossible.

I first came face-to-face with a manatee in 1972 while working on a story for Florida Sportsman magazine. The encounter was a sad experience.

I was snorkeling in the clear spring run at Blue Spring near Orange City before Blue Spring became a state park.

Blue Spring on a winter weekend today. Manatees now have the exclusive right-of-way.

The spring run, only about a third of a mile long and connected to the busy St. John's River, was often clogged with boats of all shapes and sizes.

Boaters understandably converged on Blue Spring to watch the manatees wintering there, but the twirling propeller blades were a hazard to any living creature, be it manatee or man.

To avoid boat collisions, both the manatees and I stayed beneath the docks. It was an eerie and sad sight to find the manatees hiding in these dark places. They had nowhere else to go. They had to remain in the warm 72-degree spring run. If they escaped to the much deeper waters of the St. Johns, the river's colder temperatures could kill them.

I became very concerned about and attached to these animals that day. I wanted to do whatever I could to help

MANATEES

them beat the odds so greatly stacked against them. As a writer/photographer, the best thing I could do was help increase public awareness and concern about these odd looking animals. It's human nature for us to protect only the things we care about.

This book is the culmination of that effort. Although it contains much of the general information currently known about manatees, the emphasis obviously is on photography. I do believe the old adage that one picture is worth a thousand words.

The black and white photographs are conversions from color slides taken over a span of 20 years. Since manatees are essentially gray in color, very little impact was lost in the conversion process. Oliver O. Young of Lakeland, FL, an incredible master of the darkroom, is responsible for creating such fine black and white prints from the slides.

I hope you enjoy viewing these pictures as much as I did taking them.

■

1

■

JUST WHAT IS A MANATEE, ANYWAY?

As estimated 55 to 60 million years ago, a four-footed mammal living in Africa and Eurasia abandoned the land for the sea. It's theorized this creature made such a dramatic shift because of increased competition for space and food.

The animal adapted well to its new marine environment, and it survived in considerable numbers from about 15 million years ago to the present. It remained an air-breathing mammal, but it became so specialized it could never return to land.

Today, the animal--whose closest modern relative is the elephant--uses a broad tail in the back for propulsion through the water, like a beaver. The front legs, no longer of any practical use, have transformed into a pair of flippers.

That, according to today's most accepted theory, is how manatees came into being. If all this sounds far-fetched, you can see for yourself the manatees' land-based heritage: examine the tips of each of the front flippers. The pectoral flippers always contain three to four vestigial fingernails that look remarkably like an elephant's. Furthermore, manatees and elephants, both herbivores which eat only

The front flippers of manatees all have three to four fingernails. Scientists say this is because the manatee, a distant relative of the elephant, was once a land-dwelling animal. The manatee in this picture is not sick; he is simply doing a barrel roll.

plants, have a similar tooth structure. The African hyrax, another plant-eating animal not much larger than a rabbit, is also a common ancestor of the manatee.

How the manatee got its name is uncertain. The term evidently has its roots in the language of the Carib Indians, for whom the Caribbean Sea is named. The Carib word "manati" means "woman's breast." Perhaps an unlikely term to apply to a marine animal, but the manatee is a mammal and its mammae do resemble those of humans. When the Spanish and Portuguese invaded the Carib Islands, they also adopted the same word but apparently thought it meant "with hands." Not an unnatural interpretation since the manatees' two front flippers are important for feeding, and

The manatee may contain an odd mixture of parts, but it enjoys a sleek, streamlined shape. It can swim in short bursts up to 15 mph.

(along with the tail) instrumental for steering while swimming. It was also nicknamed "sea cow" because of its preference for plants.

Florida has the only resident population of manatees remaining in the United States. In summer, Florida's manatees may range as far north as the Carolinas and as far west as Louisiana. As the weather turns cooler, manatees--like a lot of other travelers--seek out the warm waters of Florida.

Evidence indicates this has been the extent of the manatee's range over the last 10,000 years, the period since the last Ice Age. Manatee remains dating back between 6,000 B.C. to 8,500 B.C. have been found in archaeological sites only in the southeastern part of the U.S.

Manatees, like whales, dolphins and seals, are marine mammals. Manatees, however, are unrelated to whales or seals, although manatees do have something of a whale's body and a seal's head. Instead, manatees along with the dugong, are classified in an order of their own called Sirenia.

Because it has different skull characteristics, the Florida manatee (*Trichechus manatus latirostris*) is considered a subspecies of the West Indian manatee (*Trichechus manatus*) which still survives off Puerto Rico, certain parts of South America, and Mexico. (The manatees sporadically seen off Texas are believed to be visitors from Mexico and not part of Florida's resident herd.)

Largest of all surviving manatee species, the West Indian manatee has three surviving relatives spread around the world. At one time, there were as many as a dozen members of the order Sirenia.

Besides the West Indian manatee, there is the Amazonian manatee (*Trichechus inunguis*), which lives only in the

The manatee's front flippers are important for steering while swimming...

fresh water upper regions of the Amazon and Orinoco Rivers; the West African manatee (*Trichechus senegalensis*), found off the west coast of Africa; and the dugong (*Dugong dugon*), scattered throughout the Indo-Pacific, primarily in northern Australian waters. At one time the dugong lived in Florida, too, but was displaced by the manatee.

Steller's sea cow, another member of the order Sirenia, lived not long ago in the Bering Sea. It was hunted to

17

...and for sweeping food into its mouth.

extinction in the 1700s. Of a huge size, it was also very different from the other sirenians in that it lived in cold water and lived on algae.

When Columbus encountered the West Indian manatee in 1493 (he was the first European to record such a sighting), he commented that these ''mermaids'' were not as handsome as they had been painted by numerous artists over the centuries. Anyone who has ever encountered a manatee would consider that to be something of an understatement.

Although some have speculated that Columbus saw not a manatee but a monk seal (another species now extinct), the manatee is credited for being the basis for the mermaid legend. Thus its scientific classification was designated as Sirenia after the sirens of mythology.

Homer's "Odyssey" describes the powerful, irresistible siren's song. Ulysses' crew had to fill their ears with warm

The manatee has a shape like a stuffed sausage with a beaver tail tacked on the end.

beeswax and Ulysses himself--who demanded to hear the siren's song--had to be tied to the mast so he would not be lured from his ship. As the enchantress Circe warned him:

"Who draws nigh them unwittingly and hears the sound of the Sirens' voice, never doth see his wife or babies stand by him on his return, nor have they joy at his coming...the Sirens enchant him with their clear song..."

Manatees obviously do not compare to such homewreckers. Although they are able to vocalize sounds underwater, certainly no one would ever call their squeals or squeaks irresistible, except perhaps another manatee. Nor would many judge a manatee's face or body to be overpoweringly alluring. Instead, the manatee's vaguely human face is often described as one only a mother could love.

MANATEES

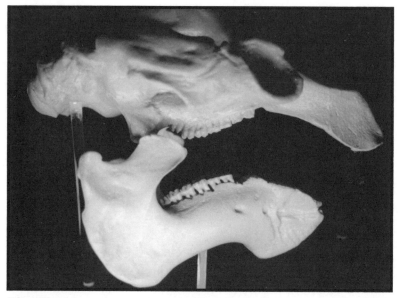

The Florida manatee is considered a subspecies of the West Indian manatee because its skull characteristics are different.

At first it is difficult to understand how any sober sailor could ever mistake the manatee for a beautiful woman unless he had been at sea for a long, long time.

A manatee's face, adorned with spiked-hair jowls, is more akin to that of a walrus than some sexy seductress. The rest of the body isn't much more alluring, either. The walrus head is tacked onto a fat, sausage-like torso, and a broad beaver's tail is attached on the other end. A pair of front flippers serve as hands. Taken as a whole, the creature appears the result of some bizarre genetic experiment.

A strange conglomeration of parts, perhaps, but the manatee enjoys a very streamlined shape. Although manatees usually cruise along at about only two miles-an-hour, their broad powerful tail can generate brief bursts of speed up to 15 miles-an-hour.

Columbus noted in his logs that mermaids were not as handsome as artists had lead him to believe.

MANATEES

A manatee's jowls are covered with short, spiked hairs; not a very kissable mermaid.

From a distance, a manatee might possibly be mistaken for a creature half-human, half-fish. When a manatee feeds, it may float vertically in the water and uses its flipper to sweep food toward its mouth. Sometimes the head and hands may bob above the waterline, which would resemble a person. When startled or frightened, a manatee slips underwater with a flip of its tail. Thus the creature could appear to have a human head and the tail of a fish.

A fully-grown manatee can be of awesome dimensions-- well over 2,000 pounds and almost 12 feet in length. The average manatee is only about 1,000 pounds, but real giants grow to a whopping 3,500 pounds.

Despite the manatee's weird appearance, there is still something majestic, almost regal, in the way these animals move and act. They move slowly, never appearing to be in

A feeding manatee bobbing on the surface, its head above the water, could make a very convincing mermaid if seen from a distance.

MANATEES

The manatee above, probably a large female, dwarfs a snorkeler. Manatees may grow to 12 to 14 feet and between 3,000 and 3,500 pounds.

any hurry. But with just a couple of flips of their tail, they can outdistance the fastest swimmer.

A manatee's face usually seems without expression, except when it yawns or readies to eat. When it opens its wide jowls, or flaps them, some observers have been unkind enough to suggest their appearance becomes grotesque. It certainly is not siren-like.

Seen underwater, the manatees' expressionless faces sometimes appear very sad, tired...almost as if the animal can foresee the fate that may await its species.

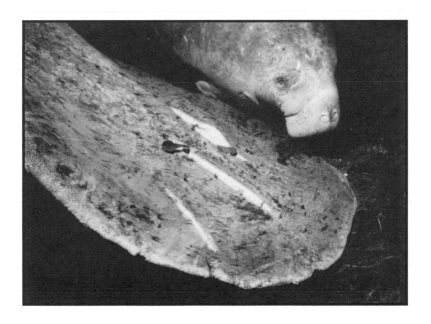

MANATEES

■

2

■

HOW MANATEES HAVE BEEN TREATED THROUGHOUT HISTORY

Manatees are fortunate to have no natural enemies in the wild. Despite their gigantic size, they are defenseless. Manatees have no claws or other weapons with which to attack or retaliate. Their teeth are suited only for grazing. Confronted by danger, their only defense is to swim away.

It is a sad but true fact: because of the manatee's size and strange looks, some people have felt compelled to spear them with pitchforks, blast them with shotguns, attack them with axes, carve their initials in them or deliberately run them down with speedboats. If manatees could be more aggressive, they might have been able to avoid some of these cruelties.

Persecution of manatees didn't start with European settlers. Indians had long considered manatee meat an excellent source of food, said to be like tender veal in texture and taste. Since the slaughter of a thousand-pound manatee could supply meat for an entire village for several days, it's easy to see why the Indians hunted the animals whenever they could.

27

MANATEES

Manatees have been hunted for food throughout history.

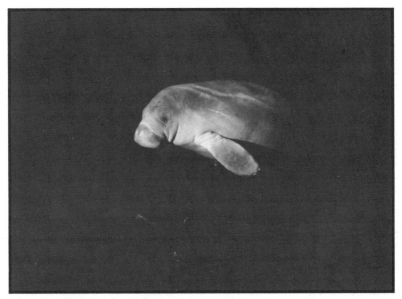

A manatee's only defense is to run away.

Not only was manatee meat tasty, it reportedly would last for as much as a year without spoiling when boiled in its own oil. Manatee oil was of such quality that some early South American missionaries preferred burning it in their lamps over the more traditional whale oil, which had a strong putrid smell.

Roman Catholics had another practical reason for liking manatees. Although Catholics were not supposed to eat meat on Friday, they were allowed to eat manatees because, technically, manatees were sea creatures. Besides the regular meat from the torso, they had the option of dining on the tail, which was eaten cold after pickled in spices for a few days.

In Florida, Seminole and Timucuan Indians harpooned manatees from canoes. It wasn't unusual for a hunter to claim a dozen of the ''big beavers'' each season. The

29

MANATEES

Manatees were once kept in pens and used for food by early Florida Keys settlers.

Spanish were willing customers for manatee meat whenever the Indians could supply it. The Indians themselves also used the bones as they would ivory.

Mexico's Maya Indians used manatee skins to make canoes and for shield coverings. In South America, the hides were made into whips for slave owners.

One of the strangest benefits of the manatee was its supposed curative power. The Spanish believed the manatee's inner ear bones were a vital ingredient for curing side pains. The bones, called stones by the Spanish, were burned and pulverized into powder. The practice was to take the powder in the morning on an empty stomach.

But not too much powder--only the amount that could be scooped up on a small coin. That was followed by a good swig of white wine. The treatment lasted for four mornings.

Before long, manatee stones were one of the New World's magic elixirs, good for almost anything that ailed you. Such as dysentery, colic and kidney problems.

Even today in parts of Central and South America the bones are worn as good luck charms against evil, to conjure up rain, and to help alleviate the pain of childbirth.

No one knows how large the manatee population was in Florida before the arrival of settlers and their guns, but it is assumed to have been sizable. Certainly, the settlers' guns made manatee killing more efficient and easier. Not all manatees were killed for food outright. At Cowpens Key in the Florida Keys, manatees were penned in a small cove to be kept alive until slaughter.

Manatees were also killed for their scientific value. Museums in the 1800s paid as much as $100 for a skeleton and another $100 for a hide. That made the manatee the most valuable animal a hunter could seek.

MANATEES

These manatees, wintering in Blue Spring State Park, are safe from persecution.

Another protected Blue Spring manatee, this one carrying a water hyacinth like a flag staff.

MANATEES

Although classified as herbivores, manatees have been known to abandon a strict vegetarian diet and eat fish.

William Bartram was the first naturalist to make a serious study of Florida's flora and fauna. His book describes his research between 1773 and 1778 and tells of a visit to what is now Manatee Springs State Park on the Gulf coast near Chiefland. The following is one of the earliest scientific descriptions of the Florida manatee:

"...the bason (sic) and stream continually peopled with prodigious numbers and variety of fish and other animals; as the alligator, and the manate (sic) or sea cow in the winter season. Part of a skeleton of one (manatee), which the Indians had killed last winter, lay upon the banks of the spring: the grinding teeth were about an inch in diameter; the ribs eighteen inches in length, and two inches and a half in thickness, bending with a gentle curve. This bone is esteemed equal to ivory. The flesh of the creature is

Manatees playfully touching.

counted wholesome and pleasant food; the Indians call them by a name which signifies the big beaver. My companion, who was a trader in the Talahasochte last winter, saw three of them at one time in this spring: they feed chiefly on aquatic grass and weeds.''

Despite everything the Florida manatee has been subjected to, it has been able to survive. Even as Bartram was writing his description at Manatee Springs, the entire population of the Steller's sea cow, the largest of the order Sirenia, was being wiped out far to the north. Also known as the Great Northern sea cow (*Hydrodamalis gigas*), the Steller's sea cow grew to an estimated 28 feet and weighed an incredible seven tons. Largest of all the sea cows and confined to the Bering Sea, it was exterminated by Russian seal hunters less than 30 years after its discovery in 1741.

The last giant sea cow was believed killed in 1768. Since the animals had no fear of man, all a hunter needed to do was walk in the water, spear one and then wait for it to die.

Remnants of the Great Northern sea cow are so rare that supposedly only a single museum in the United States has a complete skeleton: Harvard University. In all the world, there are said to be only 10 such skeletons.

However, sailors have occasionally reported sightings of giant sea cows. It is possible, though not probable, that a colony of Steller's sea cow could still have survived to this day. These tales, at least, allow it to live on in our imaginations, if nowhere else.

■

3

■

WHY MANATEES
ARE IN PERIL TODAY

Some scientists claim that Florida's population of sea cows--estimated between 1,800 and 2,200 animals--could one day soon be reduced so low that the species could never recover.

It is sadly ironic that in our lifetime--during the initial conquest of space--the manatee may be evolving into a living fossil.

An average of 85 to 90 manatees die every year. It's believed the manatee birth rate is roughly around this same figure, though no one knows for certain. Manatees spend most of the year dispersed throughout the state in dark waters which make observation and visual tracking impossible. An aerial census can be taken only during cold weather when manatees congregate in spring runs (which stay a constant 72 to 74 degrees) or around the warm water discharge areas of electrical power plants.

That's why estimates of the manatee population have changed so dramatically. In the 1970s, it was believed only 800 to 1,200 of the animals existed. Now another thousand animals have been added to the count. Does that mean the

Refuse can severely injure manatees. The right front flipper of this adult was almost severed by discarded fishing line or a crab pot float line.

This manatee calf has a damaged front flipper that is remarkably similar to the manatee on page 38. Fortunately, the cut is not as deep.

MANATEES

Manatees are attracted to the warm water outfalls of power plants during winter.

population is growing? Probably not. Instead, the increased numbers likely reflect the more accurate counting techniques available today.

Cold weather is one of the greatest threats to manatees. In spite of their blubbery appearance, manatees do not have a thick fat layer to insulate them from the cold. They may seem fat, dumpy and flaccid, but manatees are actually very muscular animals. They normally seek out their winter sites when the water temperature drops below 68 degrees, which typically occurs around mid-November.

Manatees who suffer prolonged exposure to water less than 60 degrees often die. At one time it was thought the cold water caused the manatees to contract pneumonia and other fatal diseases. The latest studies suggest that

The best time to see manatees in large numbers is when they congregate in their warm water refuges. During the day they sometimes move in groups on the surface...

something else may be at work. For a marine mammal, manatees have a low metabolic rate. A low metabolic rate is well suited for warm water--but not for cold. During harsh Florida winters, manatees may not be able to produce enough body heat to replace what is being drained away by the cold water. In humans, this condition is known as hypothermia and eventually results in death.

It's possible that manatees succumb to cold for a somewhat similar reason. Manatees apparently become very lethargic when cold catches them away from a warm water zone, and they stop eating. Without food to keep their metabolism at peak production, manatees are unable to survive. This apparently is why manatees with no visible

MANATEES

. ...*but you can be certain to find them on the bottom, stacked together like cord wood.*

42

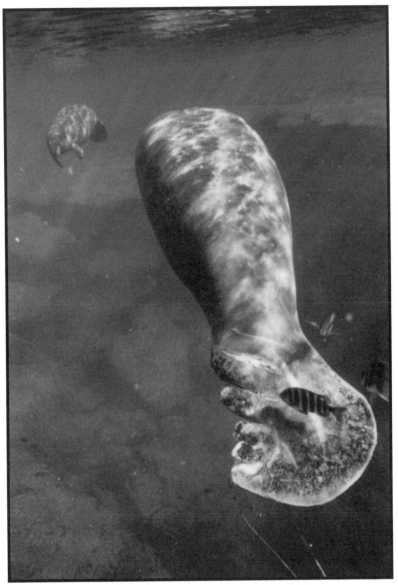

Almost all boat-manatee collisions are accidental.

Manatees lack a thick layer of fat, so deep damage to their torsos can often be fatal. This manatee, happily, survived because the cuts were not too deep.

signs of injury are often found floating, dead, after cold snaps.

Ironically, power plants may have contributed to increased deaths. Historically, manatees wintered at the southern tip of Florida or in selected natural spring runs. Construction of power plants has allowed manatees to winter farther north. Unfortunately, some plants are in the middle of the state's most developed regions, and therefore totally lacking in forage areas. That requires manatees to go for long periods of time without food during severe cold spells. Then, afterwards, they have to expend considerable energy when they are able to leave to feed on warm days; all of which stresses the animals considerably.

Manatees are at their most vulnerable when they rise to the surface to breathe.

However, it is the wide-spread loss of the all-important grazing and breeding grounds that makes manatee survival so precarious. Biologists say that as much as 80 percent of the seagrass beds manatees once depended on have been destroyed since 1960.

This has occurred not just from dredging and filling projects but the runoffs of pesticides, oil from roadways and other toxic substances. At the same time, about a thousand people a day move into Florida, and between 80 to 90 percent of new residents move near the coast. That means more people, more development, more runoff, more problems for manatees.

Fishing is one of the most popular outdoor activities in Florida. One of the best zones to fish are the estuaries and

Radio tracking collars are one way scientists track manatee movement over the course of a year.

grass flats because they are so rich in marine life. Unfortunately, those are also the manatees' grazing and breeding grounds.

For the first time in history, manatees are facing competition from another species: not for the same food, but for the same space.

In Florida, as in so many other parts of the world, human overpopulation is having a tremendous impact. Since the state encourages this continual flow of human tide, it is unrealistic to expect the situation will change for the better anytime soon.

Worst of all, most of the manatee's vital coastal habitat is already destroyed, and it's unlikely much of it will ever be replaced. As one expert has noted, what is gone is probably gone for good.

Some scientists advise that wide-scale habitat restoration is not feasible, but that restoring feeding areas near the manatees' winter refuges is quite practical. In fact, there are those who believe this is the only long-range salvation for Florida's manatees.

Unfortunately, the state of Florida is not noted for properly funding many vital services--such as road construction and education--for even its human inhabitants. Roads and schools can always be built at a later time. If something isn't done to help restore areas of manatee habitat on a large scale, there won't be any "later" for Florida's mermaids.

If habitat restoration appears bleak, several important developments in other areas add some brightness to the manatees' future. Flood control gates and canal locks in water management areas were once responsible for a considerable number of manatee deaths each year. New modifications in the structures have lessened the fatalities.

No-wake zones in some coastal areas remind boaters to keep their eyes open for manatees surfacing for air.

In addition, the hoop nets of commercial fishermen on the St. Johns River have been improved. An excluder device now in use prevents manatee calves from becoming entangled and drowning as before. Further, more protected zones that limit boaters to no-wake speeds where manatees congregate in winter have been added.

Such efforts obviously keep the manatees' future from appearing totally dismal. Yet more needs to be done.

■

4

■

MANATEE MORALS
AND MANNERS

As a mammal, manatees must rise to the surface periodically to breathe. This may be as short as every four to five minutes, or as long as ten to fifteen minutes.

Often it is only the tip of the manatee's nose that is exposed above the surface. Or the manatee may be floating just a few feet below the waterline--too low to be seen, but not low enough to escape the propeller blades. The manatee's gray color can make it almost impossible to see from the surface.

The worst problem of an approaching boat--as any scuba diver will tell you--is that, underwater, the sound of an engine seems to come from all directions. It's impossible for most divers to know the direction a boat is coming from, or its precise location, until they actually see the craft.

The ears of a manatee are not all that obvious: the ears are situated just behind their eyes but lack external ear lobes. Manatees appear to have trouble pinpointing a boat's exact location, just as divers do. It's a tragic fact that all manatees who live in the wild soon acquire scars and other markings from collisions with boats. Scar patterns, in

MANATEES

Manatees breathe through their nostrils...

fact, are how scientists identify and keep track of manatees in clear spring waters when the manatees winter over.

Each time a manatee surfaces, its two great nostrils open and the animal sucks air in, sounding much like a dolphin. When it dives, the nostrils close. As with most marine mammals, the manatee's heartbeat slows when it submerges, decreasing from 50 to 60 beats per minute to around 30. Although able to dive as much as 30 feet, manatees typically don't go much deeper than 10. Inner membranes protect their eyes.

Manatees seem to expend almost no energy when hour after hour they rest on the bottom and continually ascend and descend to breathe. When coming up for air, they seem to float upward on an invisible elevator, barely moving their bodies, until they flip their broad tail to raise their nostrils above the waterline.

. ...*not their mouths.*

Manatees lack external ear lobes. Their ear opening is located behind their eyes: can you find it?

A single manatee comes up for air while the others engage in a favorite winter time activity: resting.

By changing the volume of air in their lungs through muscular contraction and relaxation, manatees achieve perfect buoyancy control. They are fortunate to have lungs (which are up to three feet long) and a diaphragm; both stretch the length of their body cavity. Scuba divers would love to maneuver as effortlessly or as well.

For most of history, manatees have enjoyed an ideal existence. They are able to move freely into all types of water--salt, fresh, muddy or clear--and live there. However, algae does sometimes grow on their skin, but the algae is often easy to slough off, thanks to the manatee's ability to continually shed its outer skin.

MANATEES

Manatees continually slough off an outer layer of skin, which helps to remove any algae that might be growing on them.

For millions of years, food for manatees was plentiful and no threats to them existed. Mostly, all manatees did was eat and sleep.

Each day manatees swallow as much as 10 percent of their body weight, which varies between 100 and 200 pounds of aquatic plants depending on the animal. They eat for between six and eight hours, then rest the remainder of the time. Forget about a moderate diet and lots of regular exercise, this routine suits their system well: manatees are believed capable of living for up to 50 to 60 years.

Actually, manatees may travel considerable distances when not confined by the cold. One manatee that winters at Blue Spring State Park (on the St. Johns River in the middle of the state) was found spending its summers in the Miami area, a considerable journey of 700 to 800 miles.

To reach the state's southern tip, the manatee had to travel up the St. Johns, enter the Atlantic at Jacksonville, then swim down the entire east coast. That's quite a trek for a power boat, much less a paddle-powered manatee.

The manatee's intelligence has long been debated. It does have a small brain, but it obviously is smart enough to seek out a safe haven if given the chance. For instance, many east coast manatees spend their summers in Brevard County in the protected waters around the Kennedy Space Center where boat traffic is severely limited.

Furthermore, winter manatee populations have increased at Blue Spring State Park and at Crystal River on the Gulf Coast since the two have gained protective status. Blue Spring routinely receives as many as 60 manatees a winter, whereas only 10 or 11 animals visited before it became a restricted park. The soaring number of animals at Crystal River has been staggering: up from 50 to 60 animals of the 1970s to well over 300 a winter! Manatees clearly appear smart enough to recognize a protected region and to use it.

Overall, the manatee population on Florida's east and west coasts seems to be fairly equal.

Furthermore, manatees are intelligent enough to take advantage of any important new food source. Water hyacinths did not exist in Florida until the end of the 1800s, when a woman from Jacksonville supposedly imported the species into the state and released the plant into the St. Johns River because she liked its purple flower. Manatees took to devouring the hyacinths which soon clogged many of Florida's waterways, but they still seem unwilling to gorge on another noxious weed that also has invaded the state: hydrilla.

Yes, manatees may eat a lot, but they are far from indiscriminate gluttons. And, unfortunately, there are not

MANATEES

This young calf looks like it has a severe case of acne.

nearly enough of them to control the constant weed proliferation in the state's waterways. It would take hundreds of thousands of manatees, if not millions, to keep the waterways clear.

Manatees were fortunate in never having to compete with other species for food. They are the only marine mammals who eat plants, and few other creatures ever were interested in dining on the turtle grass, water hyacinth, or any of the other submerged or floating plants that manatees favor.

A manatee sometimes is willing to expend extra energy if it spots choicer plants growing at the water's edge: manatees have been seen pushing themselves partly out of the water and onto a riverbank to reach an irresistible succulent.

Give them a safe refuge and the manatees will come.

Like many vegetarians, manatees may also cheat on their diet. They are known to eat fish in the wild and will consume them in captivity.

The manatee digestive system is similar to that of other herbivores who must break down massive quantities of low protein plants. The manatee's digestive system is massive: the intestines in an adult may be as long as 130 feet.

Manatees do have one eating habit that some people might prefer never to witness. Since plants contain a high fiber content, manatees frequently eliminate their waste, which other manatees will sometimes chew.

As herbivores which sometimes have to root their food out of the bottom, manatees pick up sand and dirt which wear down their teeth. Without teeth to chew their food, manatees--or any other creature living in the wild--can't live for very long.

57

MANATEES

As a comparison, there once were Indians in New Mexico who mashed corn and other food in bowls of stone. Grit from the soft stone would mix with the food; in turn, the grit would wear down the Indians' teeth. This is one reason people from this tribe died at an early age: not from disease or war, but the simple inability to chew their food.

Manatees resolved their situation splendidly. Like sharks, manatees continually replace their teeth. New teeth move forward from the back of the mouth as needed. Consequently, the rear molars that do most of the grinding are always the sharpest teeth. Once the food and grit are passed into the stomach, a digestive produces mucous to protect the digestive system from sand, dirt and other harsh items.

The ability to replace teeth is rare among mammals. Most mammals, including us, normally grow a set of baby (milk) teeth which fall out, to be replaced by a one-time, permanent set of adult teeth.

With so many inherent advantages, it's no wonder manatees became the "lazies" of the marine mammal world. Survival was so effortless and uncomplicated that manatees never needed to create a complex social structure like other species (especially ourselves). For instance, when manatees gather together, one animal does not attempt to dominate

cont'd. on page 73

Manatee Feeding Etiquette
A Photo Essay
The following 15 pages of exquisite underwater photos explore the feeding manners and morals of the manatee.

This manatee almost appears to be inspecting its food before taking a bite.

This manatee is using its front flippers to get its body into position below the water hyacinth.

Now he rises slowly to the surface...

...for a first taste...

Our Vanishing Mermaids

...a first bite...

MANATEES

. ...*another bite*...

Manatees often prefer to eat below the waterline...

...therefore, they use their flippers to take their food underwater.

Once a plant is in a manatee's grip...

. ...*it's not likely to escape.*

Through a water hyacinth, kindly.

MANATEES

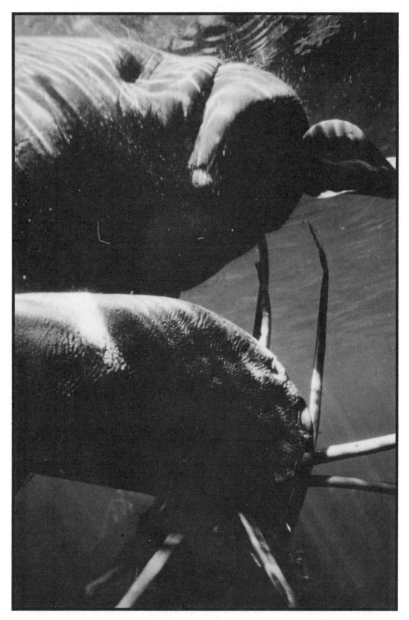

A manatee's flippers enable it to maneuver its food deftly.

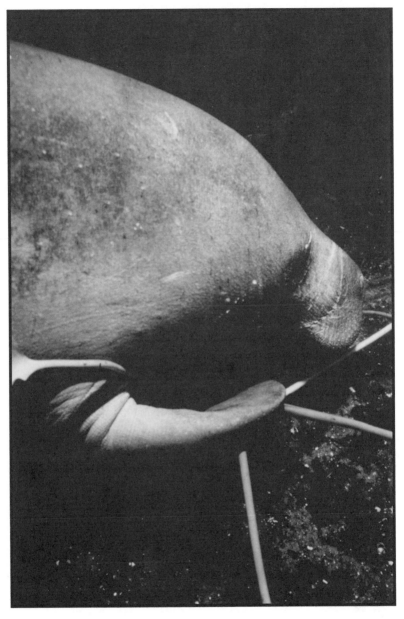

Manatees will sometimes even hold their food on the bottom.

MANATEES

Unlike many animals, manatees are not normally aggressive or territorial when it comes to food.

Manatees sometimes even share the same plant.

or boss the others. Nor do they stake out their territory to defend against others. The latest research suggests manatees abide by a genuine live-and-let-live philosophy.

The most complex interaction in the manatee world occurs between a calf and its mother. Newborn manatee calves, which may be as much as four feet long and weigh between 60 to 80 pounds, are immediately able to swim and begin nursing just a few hours after birth. They nurse underwater (or at the surface) by suckling the mother's teats which are located at the base of her flippers; the point where the flippers connect to the torso. The calves don't just take a quick gulp of milk but affix themselves for several minutes at a time.

Manatee calves remain almost constantly at their mother's side for about two years. It is up to the mother to teach the young animal the simple but all-important survival

Manatees sometimes grub for food in the bottom. Sand and dirt wears down their teeth, but manatees are able to continually replace their teeth.

lessons: migratory patterns, location of the feeding grounds, and winter refuge sites.

Manatee mothers and calves frequently touch. Body contact is considered one of the most important forms of manatee communication. The animals touch each other with their flippers, or nuzzle nose to nose, which some observers have likened to "kissing." Adults also nuzzle one another, which may be a way of saying hello or identifying each other.

Manatees also communicate by squeals and squeaks. Mothers up to 200 feet away have been known to respond at top speed to their calf's squeal: there are few things more formidable-looking underwater than watching a 3,000 pound mother streak like a torpedo to her calf's side.

The head and mouth of a manatee. Note the largest teeth are at the rear of the mouth, where most of the food grinding takes place.

Because manatees also emit sounds not audible to the human ear, a few scientists have speculated that manatees, like dolphins, may employ echolocation for communication and to find their way in murky, black water. Therefore, some scientists have described the hairs on a manatee's body as sensors which allow the animal to react to any movement in the water.

That may be wishful thinking, and the theory is not generally accepted. The obvious question: if manatees are so perceptive, why don't they stay out of the way of boats? And why do the manatees bump into things underwater? Certainly these instances would be the best time for them to employ echolocation if it truly existed.

Manatees, however, may see well up to a hundred feet in clear water. It's not known whether they see in color.

Because the mother's survival knowledge can be learned only in the wild, captive breeding and release programs do

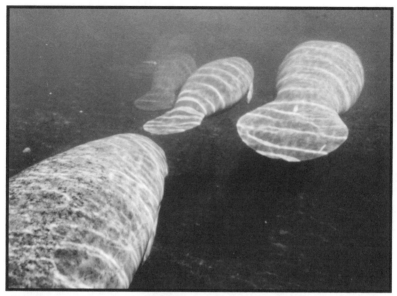

Manatees can move quickly if the need arises...

...however, relaxation seems to be their favorite activity.

The most complex interaction in the manatee world is between mother and calf.

One way to distinguish a female manatee: females have a pronounced teat just behind their front flippers.

not seem feasible for manatees. For instance, two manatees born at Miami's Seaquarium were transferred to holding pens at Homosassa Springs for almost two years to give them time to adapt to a real-world environment.

When the animals were released into the Homosassa River, which flows into the Gulf of Mexico, contact with the manatees was lost within two weeks, even though both wore radio tracking collars. The collars were later recovered. The manatees were never seen again.

It's been speculated that since the two animals never had the benefit of the normal mother-calf guidance, the manatees after release simply couldn't cope on their own. They may not have known precisely where to go or what dangers to avoid. Consequently, manatees which are raised in captive situations probably will be dependent on human welfare all of their lives.

This mother is rolling on her side to make it easier for her calf to suckle.

At the same time, captive breeding programs for replenishing the species have always been considered impractical. Females, which normally have only a single calf though twins are possible, do not become sexually mature until they are seven or eight years old; for males, sexual maturity is around nine or 10. Because of the two-year training period for each calf, females produce calves only every three to five years. Their gestation period is about 13 months. This slow reproductive rate is another reason why manatees are so endangered.

Although manatees seem little troubled by each other's company when they herd together into winter refuge sites, they normally lead a solitary life. The mother-calf relationship is an important exception.

So, too, is when a herd of males converge around a female and attempt to mate with her. A mating herd of males can demonstrate exceptional vigor in their pursuit, but it is the female who decides when, to whom and the

Mother and calf stay together for as long as two years.

number of bulls to be receptive to. A female may mate with one or more male bulls. When she joins with a male, she typically assumes the top position as the animals come together, abdomen to abdomen.

To increase their chances, groups of males will sometimes circuit broad areas searching for receptive females. Females, on the other hand, tend to stay in a relatively limited area. They simply wait for the bulls to show up. When it comes to mating, it's speculated the male manatees may possibly establish a kind of "rights of dominance" according to maturity (and possibly persistence?). It appears this is the only time when dominance is asserted among manatees.

Incidentally, how can you tell whether a manatee is male or female? You can't unless you can examine the abdominal area, the only place (to human eyes, at least) that male and female manatees are distinguishably different. A female's

It is up to the mother to train the calf in survival techniques, such as finding winter refuges.

Manatees raised in captivity are doomed without the normal mother/calf relationship. This is why captive breeding programs will not work for manatees.

genital opening is near her anal area, while a male's genitals are located more midway down his abdomen and well forward of his anal region. And, of course, the female has a nipple beneath each of her front flippers.

Despite the intensive study efforts on the manatees' lifecycle since the 1970s, much about them is still not known. Although manatees seem able to live quite comfortably in both salt and fresh water, it's still not completely understood whether they need to drink fresh water regularly in order to stay healthy.

Manatees have been known to show up at boat docks in order to drink from a fresh water hose; they will even drink from sewage outfalls. Obviously, there are still some essential facts about the manatee yet to be discovered.

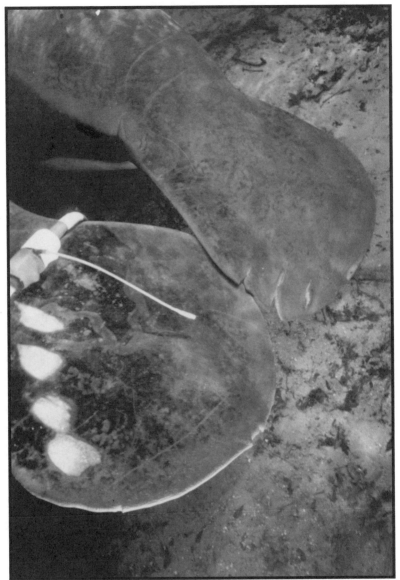

Touching is an important form of manatee communication. The manatee on the left, wearing a radio tracking collar, bears four scars on its tail. The manatee on the right has several tail lacerations.

Is this a comfortable sleeping position? At least you know where your partner is!

Manatees do indeed sometimes seem to play...

...like doing a barrel roll just for the fun of it...

..or sneaking up on food.

The life of a manatee is normally a solitary one.

This pudgy calf weighed about 70 pounds at birth and will live off mother's milk during its first few months.

■

5

■

WHERE TO SEE MANATEES

Crystal River

Snorkeling in the cool spring waters of Florida's Crystal River, I could see a pair of mermaids straight ahead, resting on the bottom. One of them, needing a breath of air, glided silently upwards. Her huge nostrils broke the surface and, sounding just like a dolphin, she loudly inhaled a deep breath. Then she sank a few feet below the waterline, gave a slow flip of her broad tail, and returned to relax on the bottom.

I've found manatees to be perfect snorkeling subjects since they spend most of their time dozing on the bottom. Their resting position is a peculiar one. Manatees don't lie flat but balance their weight on their head and tail only, and bend in the middle like a bow. It seems an awkward pose that would seem to require considerable effort but obviously not.

It is always an eerie feeling to realize I may be watching a living fossil, a species in danger of joining the dinosaur and the mastodon as part of earth's past.

Although some manatees are shy and reclusive, many actually seek out the company of snorkelers and like to

MANATEES

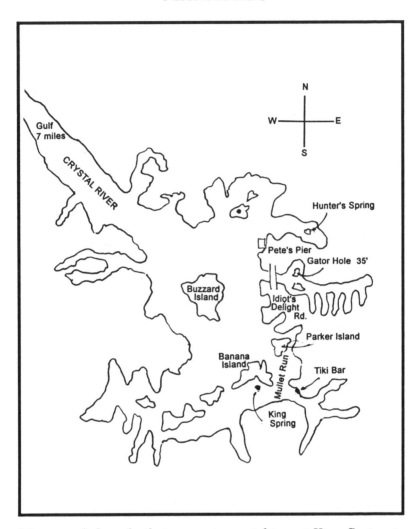

Most snorkelers do their manatee watching at King Spring in front of Banana Island.

Manatees are favorite photo subjects at Crystal River. Some animals obviously enjoy posing.

play. You can tell when you've become friends with a manatee: he'll nudge you to have you scratch his head, or do a barrel roll and stand on his head so you can scratch his stomach. Like dogs, manatees sometimes want to be gently petted.

Once you've gained an animal's confidence, it may follow you around like a puppy. I've had many follow me around and almost demanded to be petted or scratched. I've even had several stand on their head to entice me to scratch their sides and stomach.

After snorkeling with manatees for more than two decades, I've learned that if I want to see a manatee up close, it's best to let the animal approach me--not for me to see how close I can get to the animal. The key element to manatee watching is always let the animal make the first move.

Manatees should never be chased or harassed. If it wanted to, this manatee could escape these snorkelers with one flip of its tail.

Otherwise, if it appears the animal is being harassed, at Crystal River a snorkeler may be slapped with a fine. Some conservationists would even like to keep snorkelers completely away from manatees, so watching the creatures is really a privilege none of us can afford to abuse.

Snorkeling is usually a surer way than scuba to see manatees. Many manatees react to scuba by rapidly disappearing. Something about the bubbles or high-frequency inhaling noise seems to disturb them greatly.

From December to mid-February, Florida's Crystal River is the only place in the world for snorkelers to swim with the West Indian manatee in relatively clear water. Crystal River and the town of the same name are located about 80 miles north of Tampa at the junction of U.S.44 and U.S. 19.

Crystal River is one of the best fresh water snorkeling sites anywhere in the world.

Typically, scores of manatees will winter over. The best time to view them is early in the morning on a cold weekday (a wet suit is mandatory). Avoid the weekend crowds of divers and fishermen. Manatees don't mind a few snorkelers at a time, but when a horde of flippered folk show up, the animals move away from the most accessible viewing areas.

Manatees are big business for the local dive shops who know precisely where the manatees are apt to be found on any given day. Dive shops also rent small john boats with engines of 10hp and under, well suited for Crystal River. When waves in the nearby Gulf of Mexico look like Alpine peaks, Crystal River has only small ripples on its surface.

Crystal River also is a giant holding pen for both fresh and salt water fish. In winter, huge schools of salt water species enter from the Gulf: rays, sharks, grouper, jacks,

MANATEES

The number of manatees wintering at Blue Spring State Park has increased four-fold in recent years.

and snook have all been sighted. Spearing is strictly prohibited.

For complete information on facilities at Crystal River, write the Crystal River Chamber of Commerce, 1801 Northwest Hwy. 19, Suite 541, Crystal River, FL 34429; or call (904) 795-3149.

Blue Spring State Park

Located two miles from Orange City near Deland, Blue Spring State Park is one of the state's most important natural manatee wintering refuges. A half-mile boardwalk skirts the length of the spring run, making this the only place in the world where a herd of thirty to forty endangered manatees can be so easily seen from land.

Platforms overlooking the clear Blue Spring run put visitors right next to the manatees.

The boardwalk, which is easily wheelchair accessible, has several platforms extended over the constant 72-degree water which provide excellent views of the manatees, who winter here from around mid-November to mid-March. The spring flows into the St. Johns River. Once the St. Johns warms up, the manatee herd disperses until the following season. Since there is no vegetation growing in the spring run, manatees sometimes make short forays into the river for food during the winter.

The best time for manatee viewing is early in the morning, shortly after the park opens, when between 25 and 40 animals rest on the bottom, rising periodically to the surface to loudly inhale breaths of fresh air.

MANATEES

The boardwalk also passes through a heavily wooded hammock and ends at the boil of Blue Spring. Fish life in the immediate vicinity of the boil is scarce, due to the water's low oxygen content. However, it can become quite abundant just a few hundred feet down the run--particularly garfish and big tilapia.

Understandably, Blue Spring is a very popular park. On weekends, be at the park soon after it opens at 8 a.m. or you may have to line up in your car outside the park until there is an empty parking space inside. Visit on a weekday if possible, realizing that even weekdays can be crowded with bus loads of school children (who typically do not arrive before 10 a.m.)

Park rangers offer special audio-visual programs when the manatees are in residence. For complete information, contact Blue Spring State Park, 2100 West French Avenue, Orange City, FL 32763; (904) 775-3663. Campsites and vacation cabins are available.

Miami Seaquarium

The Miami Seaquarium, which has participated in the recovery and rehabilitation of more than 65 manatees, also houses the most prolific manatee breeding colony anywhere in the U.S.

One of the Seaquarium's most famous charges was "Sewer Sam," who received his unusual name after being removed from a storm drain that he'd been wedged in for several days. His recovery, which included a diet of 100 pounds of iceberg lettuce daily, lasted almost two years.

Stories about Sam appeared all over the world, but what ensured a lasting claim to fame was the filming of his release in 1971 by Jacques Cousteau. Before being set free, Sam was taken to Crystal River and allowed to readjust to the

The Miami Seaquarium brings in an injured manatee for treatment. Photo copyright Miami Seaquarium.

wild. When finally allowed let loose, he was at first reluctant to leave. When Sam did depart after a few days, he was never seen again. Cousteau's "Undersea World" program on manatees was one of the first to focus on the manatees' plight.

Miami Seaquarium's oldest resident is Juliet, who has been living at the Seaquarium since the 1950s.

Despite her advanced age, Juliet has stayed sexually active. She last gave birth to a healthy calf in March, 1993. A few months later, Juliet went on to nurse another baby manatee hundreds of miles away.

A half-cup of Juliet's milk was airlifted from Miami to La Parguera, Puerto Rico, to help an orphaned calf fight off a severe infection. The milk, with its normal antibodies for

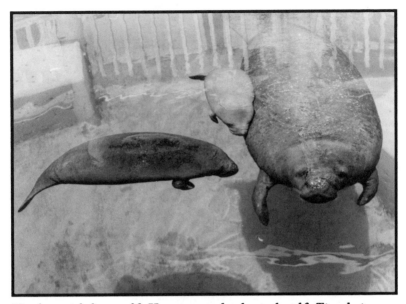

Naples with her calf, Harvey, and adopted calf, Timehri.

Photo copyright Miami Seaquarium.

fighting off infection, was intended to be mixed with antibiotics in a special formula and fed to the sick calf seven times daily.

Over the years, Seaquarium researchers have found that the manatee's immune system is more developed than for most animals. "It is for this reason that manatees are able to survive swimming in bodies of water like the Miami River," says Dr. Gregory Bossart, the marine park's chief veterinarian.

Numerous incidents at the Miami Seaquarium continually demonstrate just how caring manatee mothers can be. For instance, a baby who suffered severe lacerations after being hit by a boat in Port Everglades was behaviorally adopted by a four-year old female who had never been a mother.

Even more remarkable is the story of Naples and Timehri. Shortly after Timehri--a three-week old calf suffering from dehydration and malnutrition--arrived at the Seaquarium, Naples gave birth to a calf of her own.

Timehri was placed in the pool with Naples and her calf. Naples immediately adopted Timehri, raising her as her own. Naples must not have ever held out on Timehri when it came to breast feeding. Within three years, Timehri weighed a hefty 1,000 pounds.

Hurricane Andrew, which in 1972 caused the worst hurricane destruction in U.S. history, had little impact on the Seaquarium's manatees. In fact, Naples gave birth to her calf just three days after Andrew struck Miami. Appropriately, the newborn female was named Andrea.

Although the Seaquarium's rehabilitation area is closed to the public, visitors can view as many as a half-dozen manatees featured in the park's 90,000 gallon Celebrity Pool, which has both above and underwater viewing. Manatee education programs are presented at the pool three times daily.

The Miami Seaquarium is located at 4400 Rickenbacker Causeway, Virginia Key, in Miami; (305) 361-5705.

Sea World of Florida

Sea World of Florida launched its Manatee Rescue and Rehabilitation program in 1976. One of the state's leading manatee rescue and rehab facilities, Sea World has been both instrumental and innovative in developing new methods for manatee recovery, especially orphans. Take the story of Violet, for example.

In August of 1980, Violet was observed swimming alone in Crystal River. She was a very young female,

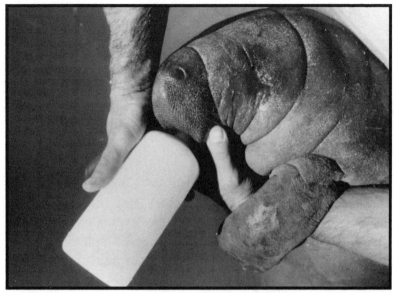

Newly orphaned Violet receiving a bottle feeding at Sea World.

probably not more than a few weeks old. Left alone without the care and protection of her mother, she would soon perish.

To determine whether she was truly abandoned, a watch was kept over her, but no other animal appeared to take interest in Violet.

Once it was decided the calf was orphaned, a call was placed to Sea World in Orlando, who dispatched a rescue team to take her to the theme park where she could be cared for in a large holding tank.

When the Sea World rescue team arrived, Violet was close to a group of boats, the most dangerous place she could have chosen. Fortunately, all the divers needed for rescue was to slip into the water, deftly raise her into the boat and transport her back to Orlando in a specially designed box.

Violet lived in a small pool when she first came to Sea World in the 1980s.

Sea World estimated Violet to be about a month old weighing about 70 pounds. Baby manatees, like other young mammals, rely on mother's milk for the first several months of their lives. Violet would have to accept a substitute in order to survive.

Even under the best circumstances that is never easy. Sea World, like all marine rescue facilities, had experienced its share of unsuccessful rescue attempts. Two other

Sea World's "Manatees: The Last Generation?" allows visitors to see manatees from both above and below the surface.

manatee calves in generally good physical condition had refused to eat and died.

Fortunately, another baby manatee named Marina had been brought to Sea World the previous year and had proven a valuable test animal for many procedures that would be used with Violet.

For instance, it was discovered that bottle feeding was a successful approach and that it was necessary to use the same kind of nipple as when nursing lambs.

A proper feeding formula was also established thanks to the earlier work with Marina. The mixture of powdered milk supplement, concentrated milk and vitamins diluted with water was as nutritious as anything a sea cow could supply. The question was: would Violet accept it?

At first, she wanted no part of it. Violet's feeding schedule soon became more harrowing for her handlers than for her. She had to be fed six times a day, beginning at 5 a.m. Rising early wasn't the most difficult part for the Sea World handlers: it was getting into the 70 degree water at 5 a.m. that was the hard part.

An assistant curator who was selected to make some of those 5 a.m. plunges recalls, "Getting into that cold water was not a lot of fun. It was always a kind of a shock at first. And the feeding was a slow process. It would usually take over an hour for Violet to finish a bottle."

Initially, as much milk ended up in the water as inside her. It required nearly two weeks of around-the-clock coaxing to convince Violet to eat.

But it worked: Violet became the first manatee in the United States to be successfully bottle raised. She demonstrated this was a workable procedure that could be used to save other orphaned, newborn calves.

After finally persuading her to take the bottle willingly, the next step was to train her to respond to some of her handler's desires. For example, it was decided the practice of getting in the water with Violet at each feeding had to end.

So, Violet was conditioned to be fed by coming over to the side of the tank at the slap of a hand. It took almost two months to complete this single training step. It might have taken longer if Marina hadn't been present to show how it should be done.

Gradually, Violet's diet changed from only milk to hydroponically grown wheat and Romaine lettuce. Romaine lettuce, one of the most expensive of all lettuces and best known as an essential ingredient for Caesar salad, is the lettuce manatees favor, apparently because it has more edible parts. (Raising manatees in captivity is expensive. The average adult eats 100 to 200 pounds of Romaine lettuce daily, which annually adds up to over $30,000.)

Unfortunately, Violet lived only for three years, but some of the knowledge gained from her rescue is still used in manatee recovery facilities throughout Florida.

Today, one of Sea World's most popular displays is the very realistic-looking ''Manatees: The Last Generation?'' a 300,000 gallon habitat made to resemble a lush tropical lagoon. Visitors can observe manatees either from the surface or enjoy a spectacular diver's-eye view of the small manatee herd through a 126-foot long acrylic panel that spans one side of the exhibit. Tarpon, snook and other fish also share the giant tank.

The Living Seas, Epcot Center

United Technology's The Living Seas at Epcot is home to a rare manatee family. The mother is Lorelei, the first manatee conceived and born in captivity. Lorelei was born at the Miami Seaquarium in 1975 and has demonstrated that life in captivity suits her well. She gave birth to her own calf in The Living Seas pavilion in 1991 on a September 13, hardly an unlucky day at all. The birth was an unusual opportunity that allowed scientists to observe the birthing process almost moment by moment. Lorelei's water broke about 4:30 p.m., but the tail of her 71-pound calf didn't appear until around 8 p.m.

Manatees have a high infant mortality rate in the wild, but mother and son did splendidly. Lorelei and son Chester bonded immediately; he began nursing within 12 hours. Lorelei seemed determine to produce a calf; she had given birth to a stillborn calf in June, 1990, then became pregnant again almost immediately.

The manatees at The Living Seas pavilion at Walt Disney World's Epcot are truly distinguished. Lorelei, the mother, was the first manatee conceived and born in captivity, at the Miami Seaquarium in 1975. Lorelei gave birth to her own calf, Chester, in the Living Seas in 1991. Photo by Walt Disney Company.

The father, Jean Pierre, himself rescued as a calf in the Intracoastal Waterway on Florida's East coast, was not present when his son was born. He had been moved to the Lowry Park Zoo in Tampa during the last stages of the 12-month pregnancy. The weight differential between mother and father before birth is interesting to note. Lorelei was 867 pounds and nine feet, four inches long. Jean Pierre, also known as J.P. and five years younger than Lorelei, was significantly slimmer at 675 pounds and a few inches shorter at nine feet in length.

The Lowry Park Zoo has one of Florida's three major manatee rehabilitation and care centers.

Lorelei and son Chester are part of the six-million gallon aquarium that is one of the world's largest. Titled the "world's sixth largest ocean," the aquarium provides the manatees a separate area of their own which allows visitors to view the animals without distraction.

Lowry Park Zoo, Tampa

Located at 7530 North Boulevard, this small 24-acre zoo is ranked one of the top three for its size by the American Association of Zoological Parks and Aquariums. With 1,600 animals representing 272 species (including 31 threatened or endangered), manatees are a main attraction.

Lowry Park's Florida Manatee Hospital and Aquatic Center is a special rescue, care and recovery facility. Animals that regain their full health are released back into the wild.

Although the aquatic center is available for viewing as part of the general admission fee, behind-the-scenes tours of the hospital are conducted Wednesday through Sunday only. (Call 813/935-8552 to make sure this schedule is unchanged.)

The Lowry Park Zoo's center is Florida's third manatee critical care facility. Like a hospital for humans, the manatee hospital provides X-ray and dark room, an operating room, and anesthesia. The center was funded by Pepsi Cola and the city of Tampa.

South Florida Museum and Bishop Planetarium

Located in Bradenton just north of Sarasota, the South Florida Museum is home to Snooty, the internationally-famous manatee raised in captivity longer than any other manatee in the world.

Snooty began life in Miami in 1948. Because his mother was injured by a boat shortly before he was born, Snooty had to begin life inside a tank, which back in the 1940's was a very dangerous place for a baby manatee. Before Snooty, every manatee ever born in captivity had died before reaching maturity.

In 1949, Snooty was moved to the town of Bradenton where he eventually became the mascot of Manatee County. Snooty's life for 17 years, from 1949 until 1966, was hardly a happy fairy tale: he lived alone in a small tank as part of the South Florida Museum.

Things took a turn much for the better in 1966 when the museum expanded and Snooty received a much larger 12 by 20-foot pool.

107

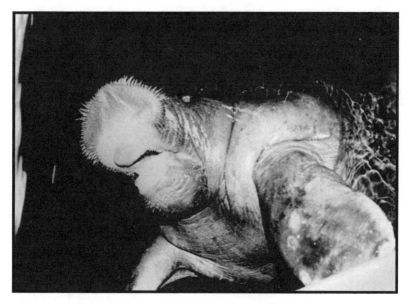

Meet world-famous Snooty. Born in 1948, he was the first manatee born in captivity. He has lived in captivity all his life, which makes Snooty the longest-living manatee raised entirely in captivity. Photo courtesy the South Florida Museum and Bishop Planetarium.

Today, the nine-foot long, 1,000-pound-plus Snooty is enjoying life as the Bishop Museum's star attraction. Over a million visitors have seen him. The Mote Marine Lab in Sarasota has used him for conducting hearing tests. And, he has become a standard part of the regular classroom curriculum for grades 1 through 3 in Manatee County.

Few manatees have ever received so much continued attention. Snooty's annual birthday party has become a major area tradition. His birthday, with free cupcakes, punch and a birthday card contest, is held the Saturday closest to July 21, his actual birthday.

In turn, Snooty shows keen interest in his visitors, sometimes using his flippers to draw himself closer to a person at the edge of his tank.

Snooty is fed periodically throughout the day. His eats between 80 and 100 pounds of food and his diet includes heads of romaine lettuce, carrots and apples. He also receives snacks of monkey chow and vitamin supplements.

Perhaps Snooty has been leading a fairy tale life after all. In the fall of 1993, Snooty moved once more, this time into even newer, more expansive quarters as part of Phase III of the museum's continued expansion. Snooty now lives in a 60,000 gallon, 40 x 25-foot pool that has both deep and shallow ends for his feeding routine, plus a meeting/ classroom for below water viewing. His new home was not inexpensive: almost $1.5 million.

Perhaps the greatest change for Snooty was that, to meet federal standards, he was given an opportunity for the company of another manatee for the first time in his life. Ironically, people have often jokingly speculated that Snooty might never have realized he was a manatee. For virtually all of his life, his only companions have been humans.

Snooty's new pool has room to provide housing for as many as three manatees. The new Manatee Education and Research Facility also displays exhibits on manatee habitat, physiology and anatomy.

Snooty, at last, has come into his own. Snooty certainly deserves ''and he lived happily ever after...''

Snooty is currently featured in formal presentations during the week at 1:00, 2:30 and 4:00 p.m.; to confirm, call (813) 746-4132. The South Florida Museum hours are 10 a.m. to 5 p.m. Tuesday through Saturday; noon to 6 p.m.

The observatory at Homosassa Springs State Wildlife Park provides above-water views as well as an underwater observatory.

Sunday. Closed Monday. The museum is located at 201 10th Street West, Bradenton.

Homosassa Springs State Wildlife Park

The most northerly of all the manatee viewing areas, this 150 acre park is at the headwaters of the crystal clear Homosassa River. It is located 75 miles north of Tampa and 90 miles northwest of Orlando near the Gulf of Mexico and the town of Homosassa.

The park has long been known for its 45-foot deep natural spring which pumps millions of gallons of water per

Homosassa is the only place you can be sure of viewing manatees in natural surroundings every day of the year.

hour. The spring is the headwaters of the Homosassa River which meanders for nine miles to enter the Gulf of Mexico.

Besides being home to as many as 34 different species of fish, the park has become an important refuge for manatees born in captivity. It also serves as a half-way house for injured manatees who can be released back into the wild. Homosassa wildlife park is the only place manatees can be seen in a natural environment year-round.

Because of its natural spring and "real world" conditions, Homosassa Springs is a favorite last stop for a manatee about to be released in the wild.

Park rangers offer educational programs on the manatees three times daily: 11:30 a.m., 1:45 p.m. and 4:15 p.m. Bleachers for these programs are next to the main spring.

Manatees can be viewed closeup, nose-to-nose through a floating underwater observatory. This 168-ton structure was built like a ship. In order not to damage the fish population, it was launched by using bananas instead of applying the usual grease to the ways. The concept may seem outlandish, but it was adapted from an old Max Sennett movie.

In addition to the manatee viewing available 365 days a year, visitors have miles of nature trails to walk and can also cruise the Pepper Creek by tour boat. The park opens daily (including holidays) at 9 a.m. and closes at 5:30 p.m. The last ticket is sold at 4 p.m.

The park entrance is a quarter mile west of U.S. 19 in Homosassa Springs. For complete information, call (904) 628-2311.

MANATEES

Tampa Electric's Manatee Viewing Center

The Big Bend Station of Tampa Electric Company is one of those warm-water discharge plants that attracts a sizable herd of manatees during winter. Although a spectacle like this might normally be off-limits, Tampa Electric has built a special manatee viewing center which includes an observation platform to view the manatees living in the discharge canal during cold weather.

The center is open only from early December through March, when manatees are most likely to be present. The size of the herd at any one time likely will be determined by how cold the weather is. Closed on Monday and Tuesday, the manatee viewing center is open Wednesday through Saturday from 10 a.m. to 5:30 p.m.; on Sunday from 1 p.m. to 5:30 p.m. The center is also open on Christmas and New Year's Day from noon to 5 p.m.

To reach the Big Bend Manatee Viewing Center, from I-75 in Tampa take the Apollo Beach exit onto Big Bend Road; go west, toward the Gulf. You will pass through a major intersection with U.S. 41; continue west on Big Bend Road for about another mile when the road turns sharply to the left. The viewing center is at this sharp turn. An information hotline with an updated recorded message is available 24-hours a day: (813) 228-4289.

Manatee Springs State Park

Located near the city of Chiefland, the first magnitude spring here produces 81,280 gallons of 72-degree water every minute that dumps into the Suwannee River, and

that's what attracts manatees from November through March. This also is the place where naturalist William Bartram wrote one of the first scientific descriptions of a manatee, in 1774 (see p. 34).

Manatee appearances are not always as consistent as at Blue Spring State Park or Crystal River, so be sure to call ahead. However, this 2,075-acre state park is one of Florida's most striking. It has several excellent nature trails plus a boardwalk that borders the spring run which is wheelchair accessible. Swimmers must leave the spring when the manatees appear. Take Alt. 27 to the city of Chiefland and look for the prominent park signs in the middle of town; you will be turning west. Telephone (904) 493-6072. Opens at 8 a.m.

Port Everglades

Fort Lauderdale's busy international shipping port is not where you'd expect to do much manatee viewing. However, the warm water discharge from the Florida Power and Electric power plant attracts quite a few manatees in cold weather, so a public observation platform has been provided for close-up manatee viewing.

Manatees are only one of the attractions at Port Everglades Ocean Life Viewing Area. You'll also get a good look at various aquatic plants and possibly spot some of the 120 different fish species that swim in over the course of a year.

From I-95 in Fort Lauderdale, take the State Road 84/ SW 24th St. exit and go east. Continue east on this road which will take you to Port Everglades itself. Go right when you reach the water and proceed to the designated parking area.

Larsen's Outdoor Publishing

RESOURCE DIRECTORY

If you are interested in more productive fishing, hunting and diving trips, this information is for you!

Learn how to be more successful on your next outdoor venture from these secrets, tips and tactics. Larsen's Outdoor Publishing offers informational-type books that focus on how and where to catch the most popular sport fish, hunt the most popular game or travel to productive or exciting destinations.

The perfect-bound, soft-cover books include numerous illustrative graphics, line drawings, maps and photographs. Many of our **LIBRARIES** are nationwide in scope. Others cover the Gulf and Atlantic coasts from Florida to Texas to Maryland and some foreign waters. One **SERIES** focuses on the top lakes, rivers and creeks in the nation's most visited largemouth bass fishing state.

> ### THANKS!
> *"I appreciate the research you've done to enhance the sport for weekend anglers."*
> *R. Willis, Jacksonville, FL*

All series appeal to outdoors readers of all skill levels. Their unique four-color cover design, interior layout, quality, information content and economical price makes these books your best source of knowledge. Best of all, you will know how to be more successful in your outdoor endeavors!!

ON VIDEO!
Lowrance Electronics Presents
ADVANCED BASS FISHING TACTICS
with Larry Larsen

(V1) This 50-minute video is dedicated to serious anglers - those who are truly interested in learning more about the sport and in catching more and larger bass each trip. Part I details how to catch more bass from aquatic vegetaion; Part II covers tips to most effectively fish docks & piers; Part III involves trolling strategies for bigger fish, and Part IV outlines using electronics to locate bass in deep waters. Don't miss this informative and entertaining opportunity where Larry shares his knowledge and expertise!

Great Tips and Tactics For The Outdoorsmen of the Nineties!

BASS SERIES LIBRARY
by Larry Larsen

(BSL1) FOLLOW THE FORAGE - BASS/PREY RELATIONSHIP - Learn how to determine dominant forage in a body of water and catch more bass!

(BSL2) VOL. 2 BETTER BASS ANGLING TECHNIQUES - Learn why one lure or bait is more successful than others and how to use each lure under varying conditions.

(BSL3) BASS PRO STRATEGIES - Professional fishermen know how changes in pH, water level, temperature and color affect bass fishing, and they know how to adapt to weather and topographical variations. Learn from their experience.

(BSL4) BASS LURES - TRICKS & TECHNIQUES - When bass become accustomed to the same artificials and presentations seen over and over again, they become harder to catch. You will learn how to modify your lures and rigs and how to develop new presentation and retrieve methods to spark the interest of largemouth!

(BSL5) SHALLOW WATER BASS - Bass spend 90% of their time in waters less than 15 feet deep. Learn productive new tactics that you can apply in marshes, estuaries, reservoirs, lakes, creeks and small ponds, and you'll triple your results!

(BSL6) BASS FISHING FACTS - Learn why and how bass behave during pre- and post-spawn, how they utilize their senses when active and how they respond to their environment, and you'll increase your bass angling success!

(BSL7) TROPHY BASS - If you're more interested in wrestling with one or two monster largemouth than with a "panful" of yearlings, then learn what techniques and locations will improve your chances.

(BSL8) ANGLER'S GUIDE TO BASS PATTERNS - Catch bass every time out by learning how to develop a productive pattern quickly and effectively. "Bass Patterns" is a reference source for all anglers, regardless of where they live or their skill level. Learn how to choose the right lure, presentation and habitat under various weather and environmental conditions!

(BSL9) BASS GUIDE TIPS - Learn secret techniques known only in a certain region or state that often work in waters all around the country. It's this new approach that usually results in excellent bass angling success. Learn how to apply what the country's top guides know!

Nine Great Volumes To Help You Catch More and Larger Bass!

(LB1) LARRY LARSEN ON BASS TACTICS

is the ultimate "how-to" book that focuses on proven productive methods. **Hundreds of highlighted tips and drawings in our LARSEN ON BASS SERIES explain how you**

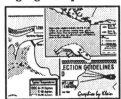

can catch more and larger bass in waters all around the country. This reference source by America's best known bass fishing writer will be invaluable to both the avid novice and expert angler!

(PF1) PEACOCK BASS EXPLOSIONS! by Larry Larsen

A must read for those anglers who are interested in catching the world's most exciting fresh water fish! Detailed tips, trip planning and tactics for peacocks in South Florida, Venezuela, Brazil, Puerto Rico, Hawaii and other destinations. This book explores the most effective tactics to take the aggressive peacock bass. You'll learn how to catch

more and larger fish using the valuable information from the author and expert angler, a four-time peacock bass world-record holder. It's the first comprehensive discussion on this wild and colorful fish.

BASS WATERS GUIDE SERIES by Larry Larsen

The most productive bass waters are described in this multi-volume series, including boat ramps, seasonal tactics, water characteristics and more. Numerous maps and photos detail specific locations.

(BW1) GUIDE TO NORTH FLORIDA BASS WATERS - Covers from Orange Lake north and west. Includes Lakes Lochloosa, Talquin and Seminole, the St. Johns, Nassau, Suwannee and Apalachicola Rivers; Newnans Lake, St. Mary's River, Juniper Lake, Ortega River, Lake Jackson, Deer Point Lake, Panhandle Mill Ponds and many more!

(BW2) GUIDE TO CENTRAL FLORIDA BASS WATERS - Covers from Tampa/Orlando to Palatka. Includes Lakes George, Rodman, Monroe, Tarpon and the Harris Chain, the St. Johns, Oklawaha and Withlacoochee Rivers, the Ocala Forest, Crystal River, Hillsborough River, Conway Chain, Homosassa River,

Lake Minneola, Lake Weir, Lake Hart, Spring Runs and many more!

(BW3) GUIDE TO SOUTH FLORIDA BASS WATERS - Covers from I-4 to the Everglades. Includes Lakes Tohopekaliga, Kissimmee, Okeechobee, Poinsett, Tenoroc and Blue Cypress, the Winter Haven Chain, Fellsmere Farm 13. Caloosahatchee River, Lake June-in-Winter, the Everglades, Lake Istokpoga, Peace River, Crooked Lake, Lake Osborne, St. Lucie Canal, Shell Creek, Lake Marian, Lake Pierce, Webb Lake and many more!

OUTDOOR TRAVEL SERIES
by M. Timothy O'Keefe and Larry Larsen

Candid guides on the best charters, time of the year, and other recommendations that can make your next fishing and/or diving trip much more enjoyable.

(OT1) FISH & DIVE THE CARIBBEAN - Vol. 1 Northern Caribbean, including Cozumel, Cayman Islands, Bahamas, Jamaica, Virgin Islands. Required reading for fishing and diving enthusiasts who want to know the most cost-effective means to enjoy these and other Caribbean islands.

(OT3) FISH & DIVE FLORIDA & The Keys - Where and how to plan a vacation to America's most popular fishing and diving destination. Features include artificial reef loran numbers; freshwater springs/caves; coral reefs/barrier islands; gulf stream/passes; inshore flats/channels; and back country estuaries.

> ### BEST BOOK CONTENT!
> *"Fish & Dive the Caribbean" was a finalist in the Best Book Content Category of the National Association of Independent Publishers (NAIP). Over 500 books were submitted by publishers including Simon & Schuster and Turner Publishing. Said the judges "An excellent source book with invaluable instructions. Written by two nationally-known experts who, indeed, know what vacationing can be!"*

DIVING SERIES by M. Timothy O'Keefe

(DL1) DIVING TO ADVENTURE shows how to get started in underwater photography, how to use current to your advantage, how to avoid seasickness, how to dive safely after dark, and how to plan a dive vacation, including live-aboard diving.

(DL2) MANATEES - OUR VANISHING MERMAIDS is an in-depth overview of nature's strangest-looking, gentlest animals. They're among America's most endangered mammals. The book covers where to see manatees while diving, why they may be living fossils, their unique life cycle, and much more.

UNCLE HOMER'S OUTDOOR CHUCKLE BOOK
by Homer Circle, Fishing Editor, Sports Afield

(OC1) In his inimitable humorous style, "Uncle Homer" relates jokes, tales, personal anecdotes and experiences covering several decades in the outdoors. These stories, memories and moments will bring grins, chuckles and deep down belly laughs as you wend your way through the folksy copy and cartoons. If you appreciate the lighter side of life, this book is a must!

OUTDOOR ADVENTURE LIBRARY
by Vin T. Sparano, Editor-in-Chief, Outdoor Life

(OA1) HUNTING DANGEROUS GAME - Live the adventure of hunting those dangerous animals that hunt back! Track a rogue elephant, survive a grizzly attack, and face a charging Cape buffalo. These classic tales will make you very nervous next time you're in the woods!

> ### KEEP ME UPDATED!
> *"I would like to get on your mailing list. I really enjoy your books!"*
> G. Granger, Cypress, CA

(OA2) GAME BIRDS & GUN DOGS - A unique collection of tales about hunters, their dogs and the upland game and waterfowl they hunt. You will read about good gun dogs and heart-breaking dogs, but never about bad dogs, because there's no such animal.

COASTAL FISHING GUIDES
by Frank Sargeant

A unique "where-to" series of detailed secret spots for Florida's finest saltwater fishing. These guide books describe hundreds of little-known honeyholes and exactly how to fish them. Prime seasons, baits and lures, marinas and dozens of detailed maps of the prime spots are included. The comprehensive index helps the reader to further pinpoint productive areas and tactics. Over $160 worth of personally-marked NOAA charts in the two books.

(FG1) FRANK SARGEANT'S SECRET SPOTS Tampa Bay to Cedar Key
Covers Hillsborough River and Davis Island through the Manatee River, Mullet Key and the Suwannee River.

(FG2) FRANK SARGEANT'S SECRET SPOTS Southwest Florida
Covers from Sarasota Bay to Marco.

INSHORE SERIES
by Frank Sargeant

(IL1) THE SNOOK BOOK-"Must" reading for anyone who loves the pursuit of this unique sub-tropic species. Every aspect of how you can find and catch big snook is covered, in all seasons and all waters where snook are found.

(IL2) THE REDFISH BOOK-Packed with expertise from the nation's leading redfish anglers and guides, this book covers every aspect of finding and fooling giant reds. You'll learn secret techniques revealed for the first time. After reading this informative book, you'll catch more redfish on your next trip!

(IL3) THE TARPON BOOK-Find and catch the wily "silver king" along the Gulf Coast, north through the mid-Atlantic, and south along Central and South American coastlines. Numerous experts share their most productive techniques.

(IL4) THE TROUT BOOK-Jammed with tips from the nation's leading trout guides and light tackle anglers. For both the old salt and the rank amateur who pursue the spotted weakfish, or seatrout, throughout the coastal waters of the Gulf and Atlantic.

HUNTING LIBRARY
by John E. Phillips

(DH1) MASTERS' SECRETS OF DEER HUNTING - Increase your deer hunting success by learning from the masters of the sport. New information on tactics and strategies is included in this book, the most comprehensive of its kind.

(DH2) THE SCIENCE OF DEER HUNTING Covers why, where and when a deer moves and deer behavior. Find the answers to many of the toughest deer hunting problems a sportsman ever encounters!

(DH3) MASTERS' SECRETS OF BOW-HUNTING DEER - Learn the skills required to take more bucks with a bow, even during gun season. A must read for those who walk into the woods with a strong bow and a swift shaft.

(TH1) MASTERS' SECRETS OF TURKEY HUNTING - Masters of the sport have solved some of the most difficult problems you can encounter while hunting wily longbeards with bows, blackpowder guns and shotguns. Learn the 10 deadly sins of turkey hunting.

RECOMMENDATION!
"Masters' Secrets of Turkey Hunting is one of the best books around. If you're looking for a good turkey book, buy it!"
J. Spencer, Stuttgart Daily Leader, AR

NO BRAGGIN'!
"From anyone else Masters' Secrets of Deer Hunting would be bragging and unbelievable. But not with John Phillips, he's paid his dues!" F. Snare, Brookville Star, OH

(BP1) BLACKPOWDER HUNTING SECRETS - Learn how to take more game during and after the season with black powder guns. If you've been hunting with black powder for years, this book will teach you better tactics to use throughout the year.

FISHING LIBRARY

(CF1) MASTERS' SECRETS OF CRAPPIE FISHING by John E. Phillips Learn how to make crappie start biting again once they have stopped, select the best jig color, find crappie in a cold front, through the ice, or in 100-degree heat. Unusual, productive crappie fishing techniques are included.

(CF2) CRAPPIE TACTICS by Larry Larsen - Whether you are a beginner or a seasoned crappie fisherman, this book will improve your catch! The book includes some basics for fun fishing, advanced techniques for year 'round crappie and tournament preparation.

CRAPPIE COUP!
"After reading your crappie book, I'm ready to overthrow the 'crappie king' at my lakeside housing development!"
R. Knorr, Haines City, FL

(CF3) MASTERS' SECRETS OF CATFISHING by John E. Phillips is your best guide to catching the best-tasting, elusive cats. If you want to know the best time of the year, the most productive places and which states to fish in your pursuit of Mr. Whiskers, then this book is for you. Special features include how to find and take monster cats, what baits to use and when, how to find a tailrace groove and more strategies for rivers or lakes.

LARSEN'S OUTDOOR PUBLISHING

CONVENIENT ORDER FORM
ALL PRICES INCLUDE POSTAGE/HANDLING

FRESH WATER

___ BSL1. Better Bass Angling Vol 1 ($11.95)
___ BSL2. Better Bass Angling Vol 2 ($11.95)
___ BSL3. Bass Pro Strategies ($11.95)
___ BSL4. Bass Lures/Techniques ($11.95)
___ BSL5. Shallow Water Bass ($11.95)
___ BSL6. Bass Fishing Facts ($11.95)
___ BSL7. Trophy Bass ($11.95)
___ BSL8. Bass Patterns ($11.95)
___ BSL9. Bass Guide Tips ($11.95)
___ CF1. Mstrs' Scrts/Crappie Fshng ($11.95)
___ CF2. Crappie Tactics ($11.95)
___ CF3. Mstr's Secrets of Catfishing ($11.95)
___ LB1. Larsen on Bass Tactics ($14.95)
___ PF1. Peacock Bass Explosions! ($14.95)

SALT WATER

___ IL1. The Snook Book ($11.95)
___ IL2. The Redfish Book ($11.95)
___ IL3. The Tarpon Book ($11.95)
___ IL4. The Trout Book ($11.95)

OTHER OUTDOORS BOOKS

___ DL1. Diving to Adventure ($11.95)
___ DL2. Manatees/Vanishing ($10.95)
___ OC1. Uncle Homer's Outdoor
Chuckle Book ($9.95)

REGIONAL

___ FG1. Secret Spots-Tampa Bay/
Cedar Key ($14.95)
___ FG2. Secret Spots - SW Florida ($14.95)
___ BW1. Guide/North Fl. Waters ($14.95)
___ BW2. Guide/Cntral Fl.Waters ($14.95)
___ BW3. Guide/South Fl.Waters ($14.95)
___ OT1. Fish/Dive - Caribbean ($13.95)
___ OT3. Fish/Dive Florida/ Keys ($13.95)

HUNTING

___ DH1. Mstrs' Secrets/ Deer Hunting ($11.95)
___ DH2. Science of Deer Hunting ($11.95)
___ DH3. Mstrs' Secrets/Bowhunting ($11.95)
___ TH1. Mstrs' Secrets/ Turkey Hunting ($11.95)
___ OA1. Hunting Dangerous Game! ($11.95)
___ OA2. Game Birds & Gun Dogs ($11.95)
___ BP1. Blackpowder Hunting Secrets ($13.95)

VIDEO &
SPECIAL DISCOUNT PACKAGES

___ V1 - Video - Advanced Bass Tactics $24.95
___ BSL - Bass Series Library (9 vol. set) $79.95
___ IL - Inshore Library (4 vol. set) $35.95
___ BW - Guides to Bass Waters (3 vols.) $37.95
Volume sets are autographed by each author.

BIG SAVINGS!
2-3 books, discount 10%
4 or more books, discount 20%

INTERNATIONAL ORDERS
Send check in U.S. funds; add
$2more per book for airmail rate

ALL PRICES INCLUDE POSTAGE/HANDLING

No. of books _____ *x $* ____ *ea = $* _____   *Special Package* ____ *@ $* _____
No. of books _____ *x $* ____ *ea = $* _____   *Special Package* ____ *@ $* _____
No. of books _____ *x $* ____ *ea = $* _____   *Video (50-min) $24.95 = $* _____
         SUBTOTAL   *$* _____   *SUBTOTAL*   *$* _____

Multi-book Discount (%) *$* _____   *(N/A on discount packages or video)*

| TOTAL ENCLOSED (check or money order) | $_____ |

NAME _____ *ADDRESS* _____

CITY _____ *STATE* _____ *ZIP* _____

Send check or Money Order to: Larsen's Outdoor Publishing, Dept. RD94
2640 Elizabeth Place, Lakeland, FL 33813 (813)644-3381

INDEX

MANATEES

Homosassa Springs State
  Wildlife Park   78, 113,
  110
hydrilla   55

I

Ice Age   16
Indians   27
Indo-Pacific   17
Intracoastal Waterway   105

J

Jacksonville   55

K

Kennedy Space Center   55

L

Living Seas at Epcot   104
Louisiana   16
Lowry Park Zoo   105, 106

M

Manatee Education and
  Research Facility   109
Manatee Hospital and Aquatic
  Center   106
Manatee Rescue and
  Rehabilitation   99
Manatee Springs State Park   34
manati   14
Maya Indians   31
Mexico   16
Miami
  Seaquarium   78, 96, 104

missionaries   29
Mote Marine Lab   108

N

New Mexico   58

O

Orange City   8, 94
Orinoco River   17

P

Pepper Creek   113
Port Everglades   98
power plants   44
Puerto Rico   16, 97

R

Resource Directory   4

S

sea cow   16
Sea World   99, 104
Seminole Indians   29
Sirenia family   16
South America   16, 31
South Florida Museum   107
Spanish   31
St. Johns River   48, 54, 95
St. John's River   9
Steller's sea cow   17, 35

T

Tampa   92, 105
Texas   16
Timucuan Indians   29

MANATEES